MW01517454

Beyond Geography

By
Stéphane Tibi

2018-19 NMI
MISSION EDUCATION RESOURCES

Books

AFRICA, O AFRICA
by Louise Robinson Chapman
Edited by Chuck and Doris Gailey

MAPS BEYOND GEOGRAPHY
by Stéphane Tibi

WHERE A YES CAN TAKE YOU
by Ramón Sierra and Juan Vásquez Pla

Maps
Beyond
Geography

By
Stéphane Tibi

◈ NAZARENE MISSIONS
INTERNATIONAL

Copyright © 2018
Nazarene Publishing House

ISBN 978-0-8341-3718-9

Printed in the United States of America

All rights reserved. No part of this publication may be reproduced, stored in a retrieval system, or transmitted in any form or by any means—for example, electronic, photocopy, recording—without the prior written permission of the publisher. The only exception is brief quotations in printed reviews.

Cover design: Darryl Bennett
Interior design: Darryl Bennett

All Scripture quotations not otherwise designated are from *The Holy Bible, New International Version*® (NIV®). Copyright © 1973, 1978, 1984, 2011 by Biblica, Inc.TM Used by permission. All rights reserved worldwide.

The World English Bible (WEB) is a 1997 revision of the American Standard Version of the Holy Bible, first published in 1901. It is in the Public Domain. Please feel free to copy and distribute it freely. Thank you to Michael Paul Johnson for making this work available. For the latest information, to report corrections, or for other correspondence, visit www.ebible.org.

Holy Bible, New Living Translation (NLT), copyright ©1996, 2004, 2007, 2013, 2015 by Tyndale House Foundation. Used by permission of Tyndale House Publishers Inc., Carol Stream, Illinois 60188. All rights reserved.

Cover Art: ocean waves designed by Freepik

Dedication

To Sandra, my dear wife, my best supporter, and most faithful companion in our pilgrimage with Jesus, our wonderful Lord and Savior.

Table of Contents

About the Author

Stéphane Tibi [STAY-fahn TEE-bee] grew up in France, a convinced atheist. He became a scientist, doing research in artificial intelligence. After becoming a Christian at the age of 25, he left his scientific work and studied theology in Switzerland and then in the USA, in Kansas City. He and his wife, Sandra [SAHN-drah], are Nazarene missionaries, having served in Africa for 10 years, and are now on the Eurasia Region.

Note on Unfamiliar or Non-English Words or Names

We celebrate the fact that the Church of the Nazarene is a global church. With that in mind, you may notice spelling, punctuation, measurements, usage, and pronunciation of words that differ from where you live. We have included the written accents and the phonetics for some names and places in keeping with the cultural preferences of those involved.

Preface

This book is about StudyMaps, a visual learning tool that was developed with the help of many people, and is used now in more than 100 countries in the world. I thank the Lord Jesus for the joyful journey thus far, and for the joy of seeing this journey continue to unfold in the coming years.

My hope and prayer is that this little book will help you see how, in our Nazarene tribe, support for the mission of God is yielding beautiful fruit across the world. These StudyMaps may be used by faithful disciples to engage more personally in missions, tell the Good News, explain our faith, and draw closer to God in prayer.

I also hope and pray that this book will challenge you to learn more about your faith and to meditate on Scripture so that you might grow in a more intimate relationship with Jesus, our wonderful Lord and Savior.

For further reference, all StudyMaps materials are available in multiple languages and free for download at www.studymaps.org. I trust that you will find them helpful and that you will use them prayerfully as you seek to share the faith and Scripture.

1 How Could I Better Learn?

First Encounter with the Bible

I would like to share a bit about my background and my first encounter with the God revealed in the Bible. This encounter changed my life and would later become instrumental in guiding me towards StudyMaps.

I grew up near Paris, France, in a family that did not believe in God. By the time I was 20 years old, I thought those who believed in God were simply weak people who were looking for crutches to walk through life. Little did I know that God would come to touch my heart and lead me to discover His love for me.

When I was studying for a master's degree in executive engineering in Paris, one of my uncles gave me a VHS tape. He told me it was a film with beautiful landscapes and an interesting political intrigue. I watched the film—Roland Joffé's [ROH-luhnd JAH-fe] *The Mission*—alone at our family house in Yerres [YEER], southeast of Paris. I was deeply touched by the beauty and love expressed in the movie. At one point in the film, a wicked mercenary repents and learns to serve and love others. A priest gives him a book, and we can hear a beautiful text. The text he read spoke about love—a humble, generous, tender love. I was so drawn to this text that I rewound the tape over and over so I could write the words down, and eventually, memorize them.

The text that touched me so deeply and would become foundational in my life was this:

Though I have all faith so that I could remove mountains and have not love, I am nothing.

And though I bestow my goods to feed the poor and though I give my body to be burned and have not love, it profits me nothing.

Love suffers long and is kind. Love envies not. Love vaunts not itself, it is not puffed up.

When I was a child, I spoke as a child, I understood as a child, I thought as a child.

But when I became a man, I put away childish things.

But now abides faith, hope, love, these three. But the greatest of these is love.

1 Corinthians 13:2b–5, 11, 13[1]

---

[1] This is the author's paraphrase of the scripture he heard in the French version of the film.

As I meditated on this text, I realized that in my own life, I had been seeking power and the praise of others. I was not humble. I was not generous. I was not tender. Instead, I was harsh, sometimes making jokes at other people's expense so I could be seen as clever. But this text spoke to what I really wanted in the depths of my heart: to learn to love and be loved.

I wanted to find where the text came from, so I went into a bookstore in Paris, found the Christian section, and finally discovered that the text was in the first epistle of Paul to the Corinthians, chapter 13. It was the first time in my life I had touched a Bible.

This was the first step of a journey that would lead me to love the stories of the Bible, to learn them, to teach them, and to become a disciple of Jesus.

After this initial encounter with the Bible, it would still take years for me to meet Christians, to begin to believe in God's existence, and to learn to pray. It was not an easy journey, but it was an immensely blessed one. This journey of discovering God's love is the best I could wish for anyone.

Struggle to Memorize Biblical Texts

As a 25-year-old and brand-new disciple of Jesus, I quickly realized that I wasn't happy with my work in artificial intelligence. Aware of the imbalance between my extensive scientific knowledge and my shallow understanding of Christianity, I began taking evening classes in theology. I prayed that God would allow me to reverse my circumstances so I could study the Bible and theology during the day, and earn money for my studies in the evening. In pursuit of this goal, I left my job and went to study theology in Fribourg [free-BUHR], Switzerland.

It was in Fribourg, with the help of a precious Bible teacher named Yohanan [yoh-hah-NAHN], that I learned much of what it means to be a disciple of Jesus. Yohanan taught me a deep love for the God of the Bible and led me to discover John Wesley's message of holiness (and later, the Holiness Movement). The fact that Yohanan was a Jew who welcomed Jesus as the Messiah was very important to me—my father was also a Jew, and I found it difficult to reconcile my Jewish heritage and the Christian faith. Yohanan helped me find peace through a deeper understanding of Scripture and a deeper relationship with Jesus.

Yohanan also helped me discover the part of the global Church where I would find my firm and joyful rooting— the Church of the Nazarene.

It was also in Fribourg that I met a young woman named Sandra who would change my life. She helped me develop my very limited relational skills and became my best friend. It was an amazing blessing when, in May 2003, Sandra agreed to marry me.

In my seven years of full-time theological studies in Switzerland, what gave me the most joy was learning to better understand the Bible by studying its books in depth and learning Hebrew and Greek.

Yet, as I tried to memorize biblical texts like the psalms or the Epistle to the Romans, I was frustrated with my weak memory. I worked very hard to memorize key chapters of Romans, but would later find that my memory was not as robust as I had hoped. I was also frustrated that after years of study, I could not remember in detail the stories of Jesus found in the Gospels.

Looking for Solutions: Visual Approaches

My frustration led me to seek better ways to learn and remember biblical texts and events of Church history in particular. For this reason, I began to review the methods of memorization used from antiquity to the 1990s.

A common factor of all the methods I studied was the use of images to strengthen the memory.

I became interested in the "loci"[LAH-chee] system in particular, which involves creating images and associating them with locations in a certain space, like a room. This "loci" system was inspired by methods used in antiquity. Scholars of the Middle Ages, such as Thomas Aquinas [uh-KWIE-nuhs] or Matteo Ricci [MAH-te-oh REE-chee], developed extensive "rooms" called "memory palaces."

Another interesting method I found was "mind maps," which combine a structured organization (like a hub and spokes of a wheel) and images to aid both memory and analysis.

One of the struggles I found was in memorizing a biblical text in different languages (French, Greek, English, and Hebrew). It was difficult to find a satisfying tool for a multilingual approach. This led me to first try developing mind maps for the verses of a psalm.

Example: A Mind Map for Psalm 23

Below is one of the first examples of a mind map I developed for a biblical text. It is not yet what would become a StudyMap (as you will discover in the next chapters), but I believe that a mind map can be a good help in memorizing a text.

Is a picture worth a thousand words? We have all heard that saying, but it implies that a picture is better than words. The truth is that, *when words and pictures are combined, both become more meaningful and more easily memorable.*

As an exercise, I invite you, if you have not already done so, to memorize Psalm 23 with the help of the associated mind map.

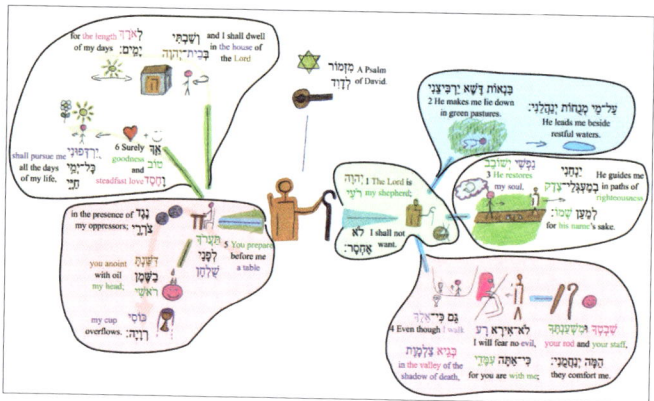

First, near the middle of the top of the graphic, the picture of a guitar serves as a reminder that this passage is a psalm (the word "psalm" essentially means "song"), and the Star of David represents David.

Verse 1 starts with a person em-
bodying the two Hebrew letters יה
which represent an abbreviation of
the name of God (sometimes written as "Yahweh" in English). This
person is holding a shepherd's staff
to represent the words "The Lord
is my shepherd." Then, on the right, a circle with a missing
part is crossed out to represent that nothing is missing, for
the text "I shall not want."

Verse 2 starts with a picture of a lamb lying in the
grass. (You can see how limited my drawing skills are.
Hopefully this will encourage you to realize you can do
better than me!) This lamb lying in the grass represents
"He makes me lie down in green pastures." The next picture is an arrow leading to a pool of water for "He leads
me beside restful waters."

Verse 3 begins with
a picture of someone
with a kind of "bubble"
on the left of the head,
which represents the

soul—for "He restores my soul." (Computer users may recognize the "Refresh" symbol inside the bubble.) The picture of God walking on a path is for "He guides me in paths of righteousness [the scales represent justice/righteousness] for his name's sake."

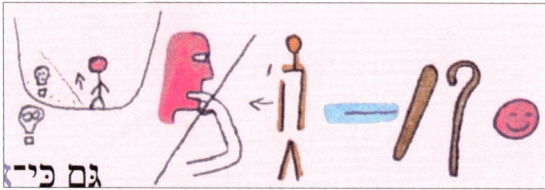

Verse 4:

- A person walking in a valley with skulls = "Even though I walk through the valley of the shadow of death"
- An image of a person putting his hand to his mouth in fear is crossed out, while God stands in front of him = "I will fear no evil, for you are with me"
- Two different staffs and a smiling face = "your rod and your staff, they comfort me"

Verse 5:

- A person sitting at a table = "You prepare before me a table"
- Two gray faces grinding their teeth = "in the presence of my oppressors"
- A smiling face with drops of oil falling on it = "you anoint my head with oil"
- An overflowing cup = "my cup overflows"

Verse 6:

- At the bottom right, a smiling face (goodness) and a heart (love) = "Surely goodness and steadfast love"
- A person in the sun (for days) and a daisy (for life) = "shall pursue me all the days of my life"
- A person turning towards a house with the symbol of God (יה) = and I shall dwell in the house of the Lord
- A sun with a double arrow (for length) = "for the length of my days"

After creating these biblical mind maps, I realized that I needed to begin developing symbols for concepts, like a sun for "days," or a daisy for "life" (reminiscent of ancient writing systems like the Egyptian hieroglyphs). These symbols would be developed more systematically in what became the StudyMaps.

2 Helping Others

Yeshivah

Yohanan was my teacher for the Introduction to the Old Testament class. What struck me was that he exemplified a living passion for knowing God through Scripture.

Growing up as a Jew, Yohanan studied three years in a Jewish school called a yeshivah [ye-SHEE-vah]. Later he was touched by the message of the gospel of Jesus and became a Christian. His teaching integrated insights from the Jewish faith for the interpretation of Scriptures. Yohanan helped me to integrate the best of the Jewish faith with a sound Christian faith.

Yohanan also showed me and my fellow students how to study Scripture in community, by asking questions concerning the biblical text of each other, and by learning to debate in a healthy and constructive way—an approach he had learned in his yeshivah. I loved this approach so much that I once attempted to enroll for the summer in a Jewish yeshivah to experience this kind of teaching firsthand, although it did not work out.

Allow me to describe what a yeshivah looks like. I followed Yohanan's advice and went to a yeshivah he recommended in eastern France. I arrived in the morning to find a large house with three floors. There, I saw students in groups of two, some with cups of coffee, discussing a page of the Talmud [TAHL-muhd]. (The Talmud is a set of books which guide the Jewish people in applying biblical principles in all the domains of life.) Throughout the day, the students would study the designated page of the Talmud for that day (called the *daf yomi* [DAHF YOH-mee]) and debate together while reading various commentators and studying different interpretations.

When they had difficulties with the meaning of a text, one student would propose a possible interpretation. The other student would then play the role of the opponent, trying to find all the weaknesses of the proposed interpretation, while the first student defended his position. Once they were done with their debate, the students would flip roles—the one defending would become the critic, and vice versa. This dialogue helped the students discern all the possible interpretations of the text and their respective values. In the process, they learned that in some cases, no single interpretation is sufficient—a realization that encouraged humility. These teams of two are called *havrouta* [hah-VROO-tah], which denotes companionship or friendship. In a yeshivah, you don't study alone but in community.

Throughout the day, the teacher, Rav Eliahou [RAHV e-lee-AH-hoo], would occasionally listen to the different groups to get an idea of the content of the discussions and discern which students were the most gifted in helping others understand. In the evening, Rav Eliahou would summarize the key points of the discussion or give corrections based on the conversations he had heard. This kind of teaching would go throughout the week, stopping shortly before the beginning of the Shabbat [shuh-BAHT] (Sabbath) on Friday afternoon.

I asked Rav Eliahou if I could come to study at the Yeshivah in the coming months. He told me to get back to him once I had studied a whole volume of the Talmud, *Berachot* [BE-rah-haht]. I did as Rav Eliahou asked, but when I contacted him again, he told me the students were on vacation, so studying with them would not be possible. In hindsight, perhaps he wasn't interested in having a Jew believing that Jesus is the Messiah join the Yeshivah.

Still, I was fascinated by the Yeshivah's method of communal learning—I found it to be efficient and simple. I learned to practice it with Yohanan, and when I became his teaching assistant in 1999, I was happy to implement it in an Old Testament class at the University of Fribourg in Switzerland.

In the coming years, I would integrate the idea of a structured page that contained all the key elements the students needed to remember for the day (like the *daf yomi*, the designated Talmud page for the day) into the methodology I would use for the StudyMaps. This format of the page would not change, which would help students associate the concepts they learned with their position in the page. This structured page would then become the foundation for the students' discussions and learning.

Let me explain more about how I began to develop this associated learning method, and how I sought to use it to help others.

Studies at NTS

At the end of 2003, Sandra and I left Switzerland for Kansas City, Missouri, USA, where I began studies at Nazarene Theological Seminary.

This was the year the French President Jacques Chirac [ZHAHK shee-RAHK] criticized George W. Bush's decision to invade Iraq—creating significant tension between the USA and France. It was also during this time that people in Washington D.C. advocated renaming French fries "freedom fries." I was glad to see the association between "French" and "freedom"—though I am not sure this was the real intention of the change!

Despite all this, Sandra and I were welcomed to the United States with grace, and we quickly fell in love with the Nazarene tribe. Roger Hahn, who was the academic dean at Nazarene Theological Seminary, invited me to his church—Kansas City First Church of the Nazarene—and I ended up going to his Sunday School class called "Times Square." Though I knew nobody there and was very introverted, a dear couple named Jim and Marolyn Miner invited me to lunch. They became like an American aunt and uncle to Sandra and me, and they often helped us understand and love the good things about American culture.

The thing that most amazed Sandra and me was that when we finally found an apartment, many people from Sunday School and others from the church collected all that we needed to move in—from chairs, to a bed, to a desk, to food in our fridge. We had never experienced such gracious and thoughtful generosity. In a touching example of incarnated love, Roger Hahn even helped me pick out our shower curtain.

Of course, I also learned much in my seminary classes—Paul Bassett, a church history teacher who later became my mentor, helped me learn the history of the Nazarene denomination with many interesting stories that will stay with me the rest of my life.

While studying, I worked in World Mission Literature (now Global Nazarene Publications) of the Nazarene headquarters with Karen Philips, who helped guide me as I served in the Global Mission Office (then called "World Mission"). My task there was to assist in delivering used books to pastors and Bible colleges around the world.

Teaching Hebrew

For our first Christmas in the US, Roger and Dorothy Hahn invited Sandra and me to have dinner with them and their family.

As a good Frenchman, I've always been very direct in speaking my mind. Sometimes I like to say that the French and the Americans are similar: In America, when someone wants to offer a criticism, they start by mentioning two or three positive points. In France, we do almost the same thing—except we don't offer the two or three positive points! With characteristic bluntness, I had told Roger Hahn that I felt the biblical languages could be taught much more efficiently through the use of pictures and interactive group-learning methods.

So, on Christmas Day 2003, Roger asked me, "Stéphane, would you be interested in teaching Hebrew at the seminary for the next year?"

I eagerly accepted the opportunity. I had already taught an advanced Hebrew class with Yohanan in Switzerland, and was very interested in the opportunity to further develop the graphic methods I was using in my own studies.

Most days, my mind was churning with ideas for graphic memorization methods. As I sought to design a way to teach the Hebrew alphabet with various mnemonics, Lindell Leatherman, a musician at Kansas City First Church, helped me discover that I could use a tune from *The Sound of Music* to do this. "Doe, a deer, a female deer…" became, "*Aleph* fishes with some *bet*…."

My first Hebrew class as a teacher started in August 2004. I knew my initial contact with the students had to be positive. If they were to be interested in my unusual methods, I needed to convince them first.

So, on the first day of class, I explained to the students that I was a scientist specialized in artificial intelligence with experience in robotics. I used as much complicated language as possible to sound very scientific. Then, I led them in singing "*Aleph* [ah-LEF] fishes with some *bet* [BAYT]." This marked a successful start to a blessed first year of teaching Hebrew with graphics. The graphics were not yet StudyMaps, but I was beginning to test and confirm the efficiency of graphic and multisensory learning methods, associated with group learning.

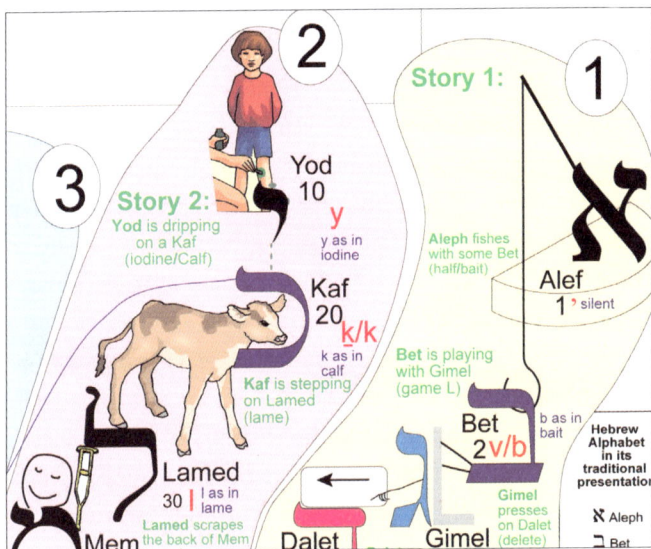

Part of the graphic I used to teach the Hebrew consonants.[2]

I also had the students meet in groups outside the classroom and work together to create visual associations for vocabulary words. For instance, for the Hebrew word *hattat* [HAHT-aht], which means "sin," one group came up with the visual association of someone shaking a burning hand

---

2   You can find the complete chart, as well as the chart for Hebrew vowels, at http://studymaps.org/Hebrew/index.html.

and saying "hot, hot" (which sounds similar to *hattat*) while pointing to a sinful situation. In this way, the students realized that, as a group, they were able to discover helpful visual associations and encourage each other. This way of developing efficient group work, sometimes called "situated learning," would later become a key part of the StudyMap learning method (see chapter 5 for more details).

My wife Sandra was one of the students in my first Hebrew class. She helped me learn how to better connect with the students and adapt my expectations when I was too demanding. One of the challenges for the students was that I spoke softly and with a strong French accent; and of course, Hebrew is a difficult subject to learn anyway. You can imagine the struggles the students had to go through to learn Hebrew from a barely understandable teacher with very unusual methods. Yet, by God's grace, the class went very well.

One of the students, Heather Bryant, enjoyed the class so much that, when she traveled to different Nazarene universities with the NTS promotion team, she encouraged all the future students to take the Hebrew class with me. This meant that in the fall 2005 semester, it was no longer 10, but 30 students who greeted me the first day of class.

First Books of the Bible

One Sunday when Roger Hahn was away, I was invited to teach his Sunday School class. Roger had been teaching on the Book of Romans for several months, so I decided to teach the key elements of each chapter of Romans using a graphic.

When Roger returned, the Sunday School class took turns joyfully repeating the content of each chapter in the Book of Romans.

Copyright © 2012 Stéphane Tibi and his licensors. All rights reserved. www.studymaps.org

3 The Articles of Faith StudyMap

Articles of Faith graphic

One day at my part-time job in the literature department, I mentioned that I was learning and teaching Hebrew using graphics. A Spanish-language editor and translator, Eduardo Aparicio [ed-WAHR-doh ah-pah-REE-see-oh], asked me if I could design a graphic for the Nazarene Articles of Faith. At his request, I created a graphic for Eduardo to use and publish.

Though it would still take years before it was fully realized, this graphic would later integrate the various features I was envisioning and become the first full-blown StudyMap.

Once, as we were visiting my family home near Paris, Sandra and I were able to use this graphic to explain the basics of the Christian faith to a dear Portuguese woman named Maria, who was helping my mother clean her house. Maria showed interest in the words we shared with her; and when we had finished, we prayed for her to welcome Jesus as her Lord and Savior and enter fully into the blessed journey of discipleship. For the first time, I realized that this graphic was more than a memory tool—it could also be a tool to share the gospel and lead people to Christ.

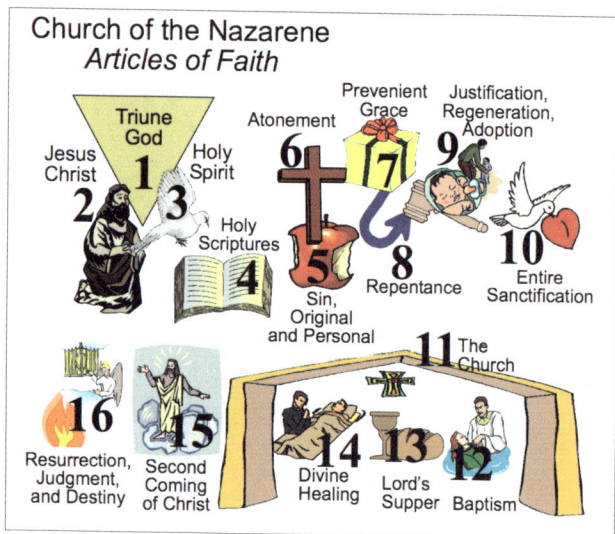

Articles of Faith graphic in its first form.

As I finished my studies at NTS and graduated with a Master of Divinity, I had the impression that the Lord wanted me to pursue a PhD. I applied to postgraduate programs, but was not accepted to any schools.

One Sunday, a dear friend from the Global Mission Department, David Hayse, called Sandra and me to ask if we would consider becoming missionaries to Rwanda. The question came as a surprise—we had never considered missionary work. When I learned about the role that France played in the Rwandan genocide, I was further discouraged from the prospect of traveling there. Sandra and I prayed about the opportunity, hoping to sense peace in refusing it. Yet, as the days went by, the Spirit convinced us to remain open to the possibility. Eventually, as we went one step at a time, we received peace in our hearts that missionary work was the Lord's will for us. We planned to arrive in Rwanda at the end of 2006. However, because of the break in diplomatic relationships with France in November 2006, we went to Uganda first, and spent the first years of our missionary service traveling regularly to Rwanda and the Democratic Republic of the Congo (DR Congo).[3]

One of the first things I did in Rwanda and the Congo was test the usefulness of the graphics on the Articles of Faith and the Gospel of Mark.

It was at this time I began looking for a name that could describe the concepts embedded in my graphics. These tools were like a map designed to help one to study, so I decided that "StudyMap" was the name that made most sense. I then registered the website studymaps.org to store these "StudyMaps."

To maximize their usefulness for discipleship and edification, these graphics were designed to be photocopied and

---

[3] There are numerous accepted abbreviations for the Democratic Republic of the Congo. "DR Congo" and "the Congo" will be used throughout the book by the author to refer to this country.

distributed freely. Eventually, the StudyMap on the Articles of Faith began to be used extensively in eastern DR Congo, with the help of two gifted teachers, Pigeon Rwananyie [PEE-jahn rwah-nah-NEE-yay] (who now serves as district superintendent of a group of churches in the north of Goma [GOH-mah]) and Deo Aluma [DAY-oh ah-LOO-mah] (a teacher from Bukavu [boo-KAH-voo] in the east of DR Congo). In eastern DR Congo, a devastating civil war began in 1996 (which, as of 2017, is still raging) and has claimed about 6 million lives. In such a difficult setting, these freely available tools helped many receive sound and simple foundations for their Christian faith. Once, when a district superintendent in this region, Célestin Chishibanji [SAY-les-tin TCHI-shi-bahn-ji], was traveling in a remote location of the Bukavu district, he was greeted by children who could recite all the Articles of Faith thanks to the Study-Map. The tool had preceded him in this area.

One of the most passionate advocates of StudyMaps was my colleague Don Gardner, who, as of 2017, still oversees our churches in Eastern Africa. He began to have the pastors on his field learn with the aid of the StudyMaps; the pastors, in turn, began to quiz each other when they met together. Once, when Don was flying from Kenya to Rwanda, he ended up sitting beside the Rwandan minister of justice. When the minister learned that Don was a missionary, he told him, "We don't need any more missionaries in Rwanda." He then asked Don how he thought the missionary work or the Church of the Nazarene could make a difference in his country. In response, Don used a napkin to sketch the StudyMap as he explained the Articles of Faith. The minister became interested, and other passengers on the plane also began to pay attention, knowing that Don was speaking to the minister of justice.

When the plane landed, the minister said, "This is the clearest explanation of the Christian faith I have ever heard. You are welcome in my country at any time. Please take my personal business card and call me if you ever need help."

Later, like Don, I also had an encounter on a plane. On a flight from New Delhi, India, to Dhaka [DAH-kah], Bangladesh, I sat next to Rosemary, who, with her husband, Amitava [ah-mee-TAH-vah], serve our churches in India and Bangladesh. In the course of our discussion, I explained to Rosemary why I had developed StudyMaps and how they could be used. I then pulled my tablet out of my bag and began to show her how to memorize and connect the Articles of Faith of our Nazarene denomination. She learned quickly and eagerly. While Rosemary and I conversed, the man in the seat next to her kept looking at the tablet. Eventually, I introduced myself to the man and began to speak with him. His name was Raj [RAZH], and he was an Indian doctor traveling to help in Bangladesh. He was not a Christian, but since I had noticed his interest in the StudyMap, I asked, "Raj, do you remember Article 5?"

He answered, "Oh, that is sin, original and personal."

"What does it mean?" I asked.

He gave me a good definition, so I asked him, "What was Article 6?"

He answered, "That is the complex word ... at-one-ment."

In about one hour, Raj had learned all the basics of the Christian faith simply by observing Rosemary and me as we used the StudyMap of the Articles of Faith. This is the heart of StudyMaps: to help people learn the foundations of the Christian faith, and thereby invite them to come closer to our loving Heavenly Father through His Son, Jesus Christ.

Challenge: Learning the Articles of Faith

I would like to challenge you to learn, with the Study-Map, the 16 Articles of Faith and to teach someone else with it.

The best way to learn is with a friend, so that you can check together that you remember well, in a playful way.

Articles of Faith artwork updated in 2017
to make the StudyMap more cross-culturally reproducible.

The first three articles describe the God we believe in.

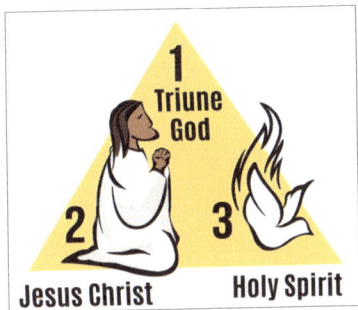

One: The Triune God

We believe in one God, who revealed himself to us as Father, Son, and Holy Spirit. He created the universe, and created humans to live in communion with Him.

Two: Jesus Christ

Jesus Christ, the Son of God, was born of the Virgin Mary. He lived His whole life in dialogue with the Father and doing His will. Jesus taught us how to enter into this relationship with God. He died on the cross for our sins, but then arose from the dead and now intercedes for us from Heaven.

Three: The Holy Spirit

The Holy Spirit is the Spirit of God that spoke through the prophets.

After His resurrection, Jesus sent the Holy Spirit to purify us and to give us the strength to love God and our neighbor. The white dove and the fire are two biblical images of the Holy Spirit, reminding us of purity and guidance (the white dove), purification and power (fire).

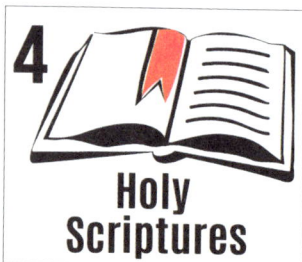

Four: The Holy Scriptures

The Holy Scriptures teach us how God invites humans into a holy relationship with Him, through faith in Jesus Christ.

Article Four acts as a bridge between the first three articles, which are about God, and Articles Five to Ten, which show the journey of humanity from sin to a perfect relationship with God.

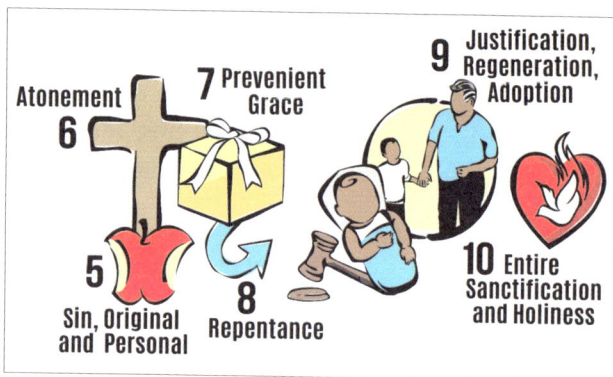

Five: Sin, Original and Personal

To sin means to miss the mark, to miss the goal. God's goal is for humans to walk with Him, to speak with Him, and to listen to and obey His loving guidance.

From the first human until now, we have disobeyed the teachings of God, thus breaking our communion with Him. The apple eaten on the two sides helps us visualize the sin of Adam and Eve on one side, and our personal sin(s) on the other side.

Six: Atonement

God sent His Son, Jesus Christ, who lived in perfect unity with Him. Jesus atoned for our sins through His death on the cross. He enabled us to be delivered from sin and to be united again with God.

Seven: Prevenient Grace

Prevenient grace is a gift from God, given before we do anything to deserve it. Through prevenient grace, God makes us aware of our sin and that we need His help in order to be delivered from our rebellious ways.

Eight: Repentance

By grace, God helps us to realize that we are separated from Him by our sinful disobedience. We need to repent, which means to turn away from sin and turn towards God, as illustrated by the turning arrow.

Nine: Justification, Regeneration, and Adoption

God grants justification to those who repent and choose to put their faith in Jesus Christ as their Lord and Savior. He forgives them and invites them to follow Jesus as their

Lord and Savior. The mallet (judge's hammer[4]) reminds us that God declares us *not guilty* when we repent and choose to trust and follow Jesus as our Lord and Savior.

Regeneration, illustrated by the picture of a baby, means to be "born again." It occurs when God justifies us, thus renewing us spiritually.

When God justifies and regenerates us, He adopts us as His children. As a loving Father, He desires to teach us His holy ways. As we listen to Him and obey Him, He will also listen to and answer our prayers. Adoption is illustrated by the image of a father with a child.

Ten: Christian Holiness and Entire Sanctification

God invites us to be entirely devoted to Him in holy obedience and perfect love. Entire sanctification happens when we consecrate ourselves fully to God. God responds by filling our hearts with His Holy Spirit, purifying us and giving us the capacity to both discern and obey His guidance in all we do. The Holy Spirit enables us not to sin, and to instead love God with all our heart, mind, and strength, and love our neighbors as ourselves. The image of a heart filled with fire and a dove (symbolizing the Holy Spirit) represents this important part of our faith.

---

[4] "Gavel" translates as "hammer" in the author's original French.

Articles Eleven to Fourteen describe the Church and three expressions of faith.

Eleven: The Church

The Church is the community of believers who confess Jesus Christ as their Savior. The Church is designed by Jesus to witness to God's love for this world. By the power of the Holy Spirit, we are invited to express this love through evangelism, discipleship, and other acts of mercy. Notice that in the image that represents this article, the bricks that comprise the church building are actually people.

Twelve: Baptism

Jesus Christ commanded us to baptize believers as a public declaration of their faith in Him as their personal Lord and Savior.

Thirteen: The Lord's Supper

Christians celebrate The Lord's Supper to proclaim the death and resurrection of our Lord Jesus Christ, as well as His abiding presence in the Church, which is the Body of Christ.

Fourteen: Divine Healing

The Bible witnesses to God's power to divinely heal sickness in response to prayer, whether through medicine or more miraculous means.

The last two articles relate to Christ's return and our final destiny.

Fifteen: Second Coming of Christ

As He promised us in the Gospels, Jesus Christ will come again.

Sixteen: Resurrection, Judgment, and Final Destiny

When Jesus comes again, there will be a resurrection of all people who have died, followed by the judgment of every human being. We will then go to our final destiny: hell for the unrepentant sinners, or eternal life for those who believed in Jesus and obediently followed Him during their lives. The person with the gray robe represents a resurrected person. The gavel (judge's hammer) illustrates the judgement, with the two possible outcomes for our destiny: hell or eternal life with God.

4 Developing the StudyMap Concept

Teaching with Graphic Tools

As I traveled throughout Central Africa teaching the Articles of Faith with the StudyMap, I also developed Study-Maps for biblical books. In 2008, I began to use the Gospel of Mark graphic in my teaching in Rwanda.

Because Mark is represented by a lion in Christian tradition, the picture in the background is a lion's head. This background image serves as a reminder of the key elements of the Gospel of Mark, as well as how those elements are connected.

Once, I traveled to Senegal to work with leaders from West and East Africa. A key

Gospel of Mark

Good News of Jesus Christ the Son of God

© 2017 Stéphane Tibi and his licensors. All rights reserved. studymaps.org

exercise during our time there was memorizing the key stories in the first chapter of the Gospel of Mark. Some of the leaders struggled with this exercise, and one day, after I'd had a difficult night with stomach pains, they prayed for a "delayed healing"—that God would heal me, but only after I had cancelled their test on the Gospel of Mark! From that experience, I learned to use a more playful and dynamic approach in teaching the Bible with StudyMaps.

About 30 percent of our brains is used for vision

Paper for the Journal *Didache*

Soon after I began using the Gospel of Mark graphic, NTS professor Dean Blevins asked if I could write a paper on StudyMaps for *Didache* [DI-dah-kay], an online scholarly journal; and I joyfully accepted. The opportunity to write the paper allowed me to clarify and explain the concepts at the root of the StudyMap approach.

Two of the key concepts in StudyMaps are *1. relative positioning* and *2. referential positioning*.

Visual memory is crucial for learning and memorization. About 30 percent of our brains is used for vision—it is by far the most complex and rich sense we possess. This means that even when we don't intend to, we integrate visual aids into our learning. For instance, when we remember a text from a physical Bible, we often remember where the text is located on the page. This can be helpful, although we generally don't remember the exact page number we're looking for and have to flip through many pages (this is where highlighting, another visual aid, can help). The advent of electronic books with variable font sizes can weaken the assistance of visual memory if we use them without other visual supports like StudyMaps.

This feature of visual memory can be called *relative positioning*: it denotes the position of text on a page or the position of an element in relationship to others. In a Study-Map on a book of the Bible, each chapter is located in a rectangle—that is, in a specific position that can be related to the other chapters. This taps into our visual memory's capacity to use relative positioning.

The second element of most StudyMaps is *referential positioning*, in which a background picture allows us to associate a part of the story with a part of the image (like the lion's head for the Gospel of Mark). There is a clear connection here with the loci method that was used in antiquity and the Middle Ages. One of the advantages with StudyMaps is that a fixed background picture is provided—this way, people don't have to create unique "rooms" or "memory palaces" in their minds as in the loci method, but can use the provided background to remember and relate key points.

By exploring the dynamics of relative and referential positioning, I was able to explain what differentiates StudyMaps from mind maps or other graphic memorization methods.

The article was published in the NTS journal *Didache*, and is available at didache.nazarene.org in Volume 8 Number 2.

Spread of StudyMaps Worldwide

The StudyMaps became a key tool promoted at the 2009 General Assembly for the Church of the Nazarene in Orlando, Florida, USA. David Hayse, the Global Nazarene Publications (GNP) director at the time, printed cards with the Articles of Faith StudyMap, as well as a large version of the Book of Romans Study-Map with a life-size Roman soldier in the background.

> The Articles of Faith StudyMap has now been translated into about 50 languages, making it the most translated piece of Nazarene literature in the world.

The Articles of Faith Study-Map has now been translated into about 50 languages, making it the most translated piece of Nazarene literature in the world. It is used for membership classes; to help Christians share their faith (sometimes with the simpler title "Basics of the Christian Faith"); to help people welcome Jesus as their Lord and Savior; for discipleship and for pastoral training. In Africa, this StudyMap has even been printed on clothing so that people can share their faith that way.

In 2009, the Africa Region developed a video using the Articles of Faith StudyMap; and in 2017, missionary Scott Stargel [STAHR-jel], current GNP director, oversaw the development of an updated video and its translation into many languages. Scott also helped oversee the most recent visual rendering of the StudyMap with graphics that are in the public domain. It is crucial to the StudyMaps project that these graphics are distributed freely and are easy to translate into any language.

Additionally, with the oversight of Global Mission Director Verne Ward, the Communications Department of the Asia-Pacific Region developed a StudyMaps app (programmed by Ernalyn Longcoop [uhr-nah-LIN LONG-koop]) that is now available for iOS and Android.

Example: The Local Nazarene Church

I would like to challenge you to use a StudyMap to learn about the key components of a Nazarene local church and how they relate. This StudyMap was developed in 2016 during an NMI leadership meeting in Johannesburg, South Africa, with the help and feedback of John Haines.

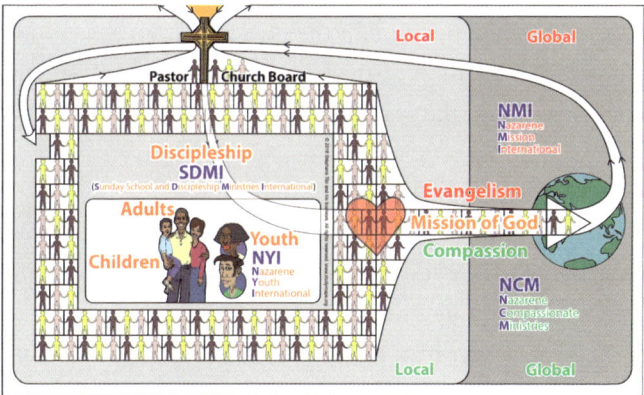

It all begins with God, who sent his beloved Son, Jesus Christ, to show us the way to the Father. Jesus came to earth and gave His life on the cross out of love for us (downward arrow to the cross), as a sacrifice for our sins.

Through His sacrifice, through His teaching, and the coming of the Holy Spirit, the Church began. That is the foundation of every local church.

The pastor and church board serve to help the members of the church maintain the direction Jesus gave to His Church. Key features of the local church are then depicted further down on the graphic.

Purpose:

The purpose of the church is to learn to become Christlike disciples. We learn from God through Scripture and follow Jesus through the guidance of the Holy Spirit in all we do. The department of the local church that oversees discipleship is called SDMI (Sunday School and Discipleship Ministries International).

Discipleship is for all ages—children, youth, and adults. NYI (Nazarene Youth International) exists to facilitate youth discipleship.

Mission:

All this is well and good, but from the very start of the Church, Jesus reminded us that the heart of His Church is love. This love burns in us through the Holy Spirit, who leads us to share this love with all we meet. This is the *Mission of God*, which can be described through two facets, that are frequently connected: *Evangelism* and *Compassion*.

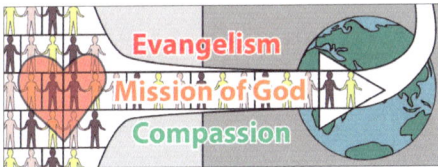

In the local church, the area of evangelism is not only for the local level but also for the global level. NMI (Nazarene

Missions International) helps each local church maintain this focus on evangelism and seeks to mobilize the church in missions, both locally and globally.

Likewise, the compassion Christ invites us to demonstrate is not only meant for those close to us, but also for people in need around the world. At the global level, NCM (Nazarene Compassionate Ministries) helps coordinate the compassionate and disaster relief efforts of each local church.

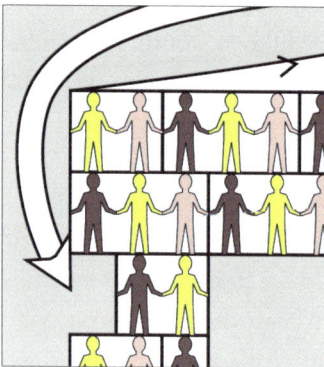

As we take God's love into the world, others will want to embrace this love and join us by becoming part of a local church. The missing person in the picture (in yellow) reminds us that there is always room for one more person in Jesus' Church—and as more people join His Church, we can live and express His holy love in this world in more and more ways

Whether at death or when He returns, all disciples of Jesus will one day be united forever with Him. The upward-pointing arrows above the cross serve to remind us of this.

Now that you have seen all the parts of this StudyMap, I challenge you to take a piece of paper and sketch out the different parts of a local Nazarene church from memory—this will help you make sure you remember all the components and how they are connected. If you don't like to draw or would rather learn with someone else, you can have a partner quiz you on the names, positions, and relationships among all the components. Do you remember what is at the heart of a local church? What is its purpose? What is its mission?

If you'd like to, you can ask knowledgeable people in your local church more about how the local church functions. This, in turn, will help you discover the crucial part you play in the wonderful Church of Jesus Christ.

Let us use this simple tool to remind each other of the amazing roles we can play in the Church of Jesus Christ, both at the local and the global levels.

5 The StudyMap Bible

Another Plane Encounter

In May 2017, on a flight from Sri Lanka to Bangalore [BAYNG-uh-lohr], I sat beside a young man named Krishna [KRISH-nah]. As we began to talk, I learned he was going to Bangalore to marry and to prepare his bride to join him in Singapore, where he worked on banking software. In the course of our discussion, he asked me what sorts of things I thought were helpful for spurring creativity. In response, I told him about the process that had led me to develop the StudyMaps.

1. The first step towards creativity, I told him, is to recognize when we are frustrated with something. In my case, I was frustrated with my poor memory of the stories of Scripture. For me as a Frenchman, this first step came almost naturally, since French culture tends to foster critical thinking. This aptitude for

critical thinking can be a negative or a positive: on the negative side, it can lead someone to quickly notice defects and become judgmental. On the positive side, noticing what is lacking can become the first step towards creativity. Perhaps this is why, in France, we have many critical and depressed people, as well as many creative people.

2. The second step towards creativity is to explore the available solutions to the problem. This exploration requires testing possible solutions, and improving them along the way. In the process of developing the StudyMaps, I began by researching various memorization methods, as mentioned in chapter 1. As I tested various methods on myself and began to see good results, the next experimental stage was to test the tools on my Hebrew students and by teaching the Articles of Faith. Then, in dialogue with the people using the graphics, I could improve and correct them.

3. Once a tool is well-tuned and useful, the third step is to convince people of the need for it. In my case, I had to lead people on a journey that began with the perception of a need that was not met. I needed to explain why the type of study methods we often use in biblical studies or in Sunday Schools are sometimes ineffective. The difficulty here was to avoid a spirit of condemnation while still emphasizing the need for better tools. I found that one of the best ways to accomplish this balance was through

empathy; by sharing my journey with others, I often found that they could identify with my desire for deeper, more accessible biblical knowledge.

4. As people become aware of the need for better solutions, a fourth step is to accompany them in experimenting with the method in question. This is what I did with my new friend Krishna on the plane. Krishna was from India, and I knew that in the schools Gandhi [GAHN-dee] had developed, students were required to memorize the Sermon on the Mount—so Krishna had at least some interest in learning more about that text. I then led him to memorize key points of Matthew 5, the first part of the Sermon on the Mount. In about 10 minutes, Krishna was able to name all the stories of Matthew 5 forward and backward. As I did with Krishna, I will invite you to memorize the key elements of Matthew 5 at the end of this chapter.

How to Visually Represent a Biblical Text

In order to develop a StudyMap for biblical texts, I had to develop a methodology that could be applied uniformly for all the books and texts of Scripture.

The approach I followed was to choose a background picture for a specific book, then position all the chapters of the book over the background picture in an organized way. In doing so, people could remember the key content of each chapter thanks to its position on the background picture, as well as its relative position to other chapters.

For instance, for the Gospel of Luke, the background picture is of Jesus offering a cup. You might remember that on the background picture, chapter 4 (which details the beginning of Jesus' ministry) is located near Jesus' mouth—you might then make the association that chapter 4 is where Jesus begins to "open the mouth" of His ministry. You can also remember the relative position of the chapters, which zig-zag from 1 to 6. Thus, the StudyMap gives two possible cues (the position on the background picture and the relative position of each chapter) to help remember the content and arrangement of each chapter.

Then, in a single chapter, there is an associated picture to represent the content of each story. For instance, for Luke 5:1–11 (calling of the first disciples), there is a picture of Jesus and a few disciples in a boat, pulling a net. Each part of the story is then grouped by verses: 1–3, 4–7, 8–10, and 11. Each of these verse groupings has a title which represents the part of the story in these verses (vv. 1–3 "Into one of the boats," vv. 4–7 "Put out into the deep," vv. 8–10 "From now on you will be catching people," v. 11 "They followed him"). People can then associate the biblical text of each verse with the circled numbers and their relative position.

They followed him 11

From now on you will be catching people 10 9 8

Into one of the boats 1 2 3

Put out into the deep 4 5 6 7

5:1-11
Jesus Calls His First Disciples

This multilayered approach allows people to remember an overall story, and then learn it in more detail. Afterwards, in recalling the story, they can navigate their memory in the same way they would navigate a map. Such a multilayered visual memory, in turn, allows people to easily connect various parts of a book to create meaningful associations. This networked memory also allows students to connect various Bible stories with the help of pictures, which fosters a theology that is deeply rooted in the stories and teachings of Scripture.

This kind of memory also allows people to access any story of the Bible easily and directly, without having to run through an entire text like they would if they only had a rote memory of the passage. This proves very important for the personal daily walk with Christ, as well as for witnessing. When the stories of Scriptures are in your heart and easily accessible, you can more easily discern which story would be helpful for the person you meet, or situation you are in, and then simply share that story or pray accordingly. In this way, Scripture and life can become more deeply connected. This helps us see the amazing value of scriptural teachings and how to live and share them with others.

The StudyMap Bible Apps

In the beginning of 2010, when I first heard about the launch of the iPad, I thought it would be the perfect support for StudyMaps, since it would allow users to zoom in and out on color graphics that could easily combine with the biblical text. In the years since, as we continue to move towards electronic texts, I have noticed that, in both good and bad ways, this technology can redefine the way we read.

> Scripture and life can become more deeply connected. This helps us see the amazing value of scriptural teachings and how to live and share them with others.

One of the great things about this technology is that it allows us to carry many books within a compact tablet or phone, which is valuable for people who travel often, including missionaries. Electronic readers also give us the ability to increase font size, which enables us to read for longer periods with less strain. One consequence of changing the size of the text, though, is that the positions of the words on the screen often move. This means that, in recalling what we've read, we may no longer remember that the text we are searching for is in the top right corner of the left page. You have probably noticed this yourself—how in your visual memory, you tend to associate a text with its position. This suggests that reading an electronic version of the Bible may make it harder to remember what we read. This is one of the many reasons why I developed the Study-Map Bible—to develop an electronic Bible that would allow readers to change the size of the font while also maintaining a visual memory aid. As the text could move, the picture remained stable.

For instance, when you read Matthew 5:13, you can associate it with the position of the salt shaker in the graphic of chapter 5, just before the light bulb for verses 14–16. The positions of the graphics in a StudyMap

Part of the StudyMap for Matthew

are fixed and do not change when you zoom in, thus providing stability for the visual memory of a text.

In my former career as an engineer, I learned to program in various languages, so I purchased a first-generation iPad and began to program for it. In 2012, I was able to publish the StudyMap Bible which combined a graphic for each book of the Bible, the biblical text in English, and in the text in the original languages (Hebrew and

Greek). We also developed a French StudyMap Bible app, a Gospel of John app with audio, and an iPhone app.

With the advent of multitasking and screen-splitting for tablets, the StudyMaps available on the studymaps.org website can be combined with any of the Bible study software or apps like Accordance,[5] Logos,[6] Olive Tree,[7] or others that function with a split screen.

The Books of the Bible

Through the years, I had developed graphics for the different books of the Bible.

Once, in 2008, I was traveling by bus with my leader, Chanshi Chanda [TCHAHN-shee TCHAHN-dah], from Burundi [boo-ROON-dee] to Rwanda. The road was bumpy, and it was lined with soldiers because of some fighting that was still taking place among armed groups. During the trip, I showed Chanshi how to use a StudyMap to learn the key message of each chapter of the Gospel of Mark. He was soon able to learn and remember the book's 16 chapters.

---

[5] Accordance is a Bible study program for Apple Macintosh, iPhone, and Windows developed by OakTree Software, Inc.

[6] Logos Bible Software is a digital library application designed for electronic Bible study. It is developed by Faithlife Corporation. As of February 2017, Logos Bible Software was in its seventh version.

[7] Olive Tree Bible Software creates biblical software and mobile apps and is an electronic publisher of Bible versions, study tools, Bible study tools, and Christian eBooks for mobile, tablet, and desktop devices. Olive Tree currently supports a variety of mobile and personal computer devices.

Afterwards, Chanshi encouraged me to use these tools throughout the Africa Central Field. So, in 2009 I presented the StudyMaps to a group of global leaders of our denomination who visited Kigali [kee-GAH-lee]. One of them, Jerry Porter, asked if I could develop a StudyMap for the whole Bible. I did so, creating a picture and a short title to describe the content of each book.

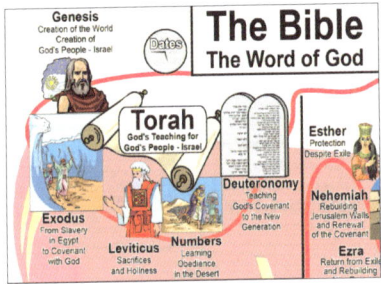

This is the section of the StudyMap that deals with the Torah [TOHR-ah] or Pentateuch [pen-tah-TOOK], the first five books of the Bible.

This graphic became the first page of the StudyMap Bible. Clicking on any one of the component images in the Torah/Pentateuch map allows users to access each book.

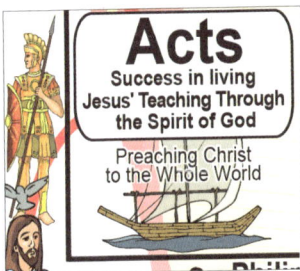

For any of these books, its component graphic would then become the background picture for the book. For instance, for the Book of Acts, the picture is a sailing boat, and you find again this picture in the background of the graphic with the 28 chapters of Acts. (Image on pg. 64)

Acts of the Apostles
Preaching Christ to the Whole World

© 2011 Brigham ... All rights reserved. www.studymap.org

1-12 The Gospel for Everyone - *Peter's Ministry*

1-5 Beginning of the Church in Jerusalem

Preparation to Receive the Holy Spirit
- 1:9-11 Jesus' Ascension
- 1:1-8 The Promise of the Holy Spirit
- 1:12-14 Praying Together
- 1:15-26 Matthias Chosen to Replace Judas

Baptism with the Holy Spirit
- 2:5-13 The Crowd Wonders
- 2:1-4 Filled with the Holy Spirit
- 2:14-36 Peter Witnesses to the Crowd
- 2:37-40 The Crowd Is Invited to Repent
- 2:41-47 A Growing and Vibrant Church

Peter witnesses of Jesus' Power and Message
- 3:1-10 Peter Heals a Crippled Beggar
- 3:11-26 Peter Witnesses in Solomon's Colonnade

6-9 First Converts in Samaria and Judea

Deacons Chosen and Stephen Arrested
- 6:1-7 Seven Chosen to Serve
- 6:8-15 Stephen Arrested

Stephen's Speech and Death
- 7:1-8 The Promise to Abraham
- 7:9-16 The Patriarchs in Egypt
- 7:17-38 God's Promise Fulfilled Through Moses
- 7:54-60 Stephen Stoned to Death
- 7:51-53 You Resist the Holy Spirit
- 7:39-43 Israel's Rebellion against God
- 7:44-50 God's True Tabernacle

Inner and Outer Challenges to the Apostolic Church
- 5:22-32 The Apostles Tried Again
- 5:33-42 Gamaliel's Advice
- 5:17-20 The Apostles Go In and Out of Prison
- 5:1-11 Ananias and Sapphira's Lie and Death
- 5:12-16 The Apostles Perform Miracles

Persecution in Jerusalem and Revival in Judea and Samaria
- Saul Begins to Destroy the Church
- 8:4-8 Philip Preaches Christ in Samaria
- 8:9-13 Simon the Sorcerer
- 8:26-40 Philip and the Ethiopian Eunuch
- 8:14-25 Simon's Sin

Impossible to Stop Peter and John
- 4:5-12 Peter and John Arrested
- 4:13-22 Forbidden to Speak in Jesus' Name
- 4:32-37 Believers Share Everything
- 4:23-31 Bold Prayer

Saul's Conversion
- 9:10-19 Ananias Heals and Baptizes Saul
- 9:20-31 Saul Preaches Christ
- 9:23-25 Saul Escapes from Damascus
- 9:26-31 Saul at Jerusalem
- 9:36-43 Peter Brings Dorcas Back to Life
- 9:32-35 Peter Heals Aeneas

10-12 First Gentile Converts

Attacks on Church Leaders and God's Protection
- 12:1-5 James Killed and Peter Imprisoned
- 12:20-25 The Death of Herod
- 12:6-19 Peter Delivered from Prison

The Message Spreads to Gentiles in Antioch
- 11:27-30 Antioch's Support in Judea's Famine
- 11:19-26 Barnabas and Saul in Antioch
- 11:1-18 Peter Justifies the Baptism of Gentiles in Jerusalem

The First Gentile Convert; Cornelius
- 10:1-8 Cornelius' Vision in Cesarea
- 10:9-16 Peter's Vision
- 10:17-23 Peter Goes Toward Cornelius' House
- 10:24-33 Peter Meets Cornelius
- 10:44-48 Gentiles Receive the Holy Spirit and Are Baptized
- 10:34-43 Peter Preaches Christ to the Gentiles in Cornelius' House

13-28 The Gospel Everywhere - *Paul's Missionary Journeys*

13-15 Paul Evangelizes in Asia Minor

Paul and Barnabas Turn to the Gentiles
- 13:1-3 Paul and Saul Sent in Mission
- 13:4-13 Paul Preaches in Cyprus
- 13:13-41 Paul Preaches in Antioch of Pisidia
- 13:42-52 Paul Turns to the Gentiles

From Iconium to Antioch
- 14:1-7 Paul and Barnabas in Iconium
- 14:8-20 Paul and Barnabas in Lystra
- 14:21-28 Return to Antioch in Syria

16-18 Paul Evangelizes in Greece

Ministry in Philippi
- 16:16-24 Paul and Silas from Exorcism to Prison
- 16:25-34 Deliverance and Jailer Saved
- 16:35-40 A Public Apology
- 16:1-5 Timothy Joins Paul and Silas
- 16:11-15 Conversion of Lydia in Philippi
- 16:6-10 Call to Macedonia

From Thessalonica to Athens
- 17:1-4 Preaching Christ in Thessalonica
- 17:5-9 Attack of Jason's House
- 17:10-15 Ministry in Berea
- 17:16-21 Paul in Athens

From Corinth to Antioch
- 17:22-34 Sermon on the Aeropagus
- 18:1-17 Paul in Corinth
- 18:18-22 Paul's Return to Antioch
- 18:24-28 Apollos' Ministry in Ephesus

Jerusalem Council for Gentile Believers
- 15:36-41 Paul Separates from Barnabas
- 15:30-35 Impact of the Letter in Antioch
- 15:6-21 The Church in Jerusalem Accepts Circumcision Uncircumcised
- 15:1-5 Dispute over Circumcision in Antioch
- 15:22-29 Letter to the Gentile Believers

19-20 Paul's Farewell Journey

Farewell to Churches in Greece and Asia
- 20:13-16 From Troas to Miletus
- 20:7-12 Eutychus' Death and Resurrection in Troas
- 20:17-38 Paul's Farewell to the Elders of Ephesus
- 20:1-6 Paul Goes Through Macedonia

Ministry and Challenges in Ephesus
- 19:1-10 Paul in Ephesus
- 19:11-20 The Sons of Sceva
- 19:21-41 The Riot in Ephesus

21-23 Paul in Jerusalem

Paul Arrested in Jerusalem
- 21:1-16 Paul Goes to Jerusalem
- 21:17-26 Paul Visits James
- 21:27-36 Paul Arrested in the Temple
- 21:37-40 Paul Asks to Speak

Paul Witnesses in Jerusalem
- 22:6-16 Paul Witnesses of His Conversion
- 22:17-21 Paul Sent to the Gentiles
- 22:1-5 Paul Defends Himself
- 22:22-30 Paul the Roman Citizen
- 23:1-11 Paul Divides the Sanhedrin over Resurrection

Paul Leaves Jerusalem for Cesarea
- 23:23-35 Paul Sent to Felix in Cesarea
- 23:12-22 The Plot Against Paul Revealed

24-26 Paul in Cesarea

Paul Witnesses to Agrippa
- 25:13-22 Paul Invites Agrippa to Faith in Jesus
- 26:24-32 Paul's Witness to Jews and Gentiles
- 26:1-11 Paul Defends Himself before Agrippa
- 26:12-18 Paul Tells of His Encounter with Christ

Paul's Appeal to Caesar and before Agrippa
- 25:23-27 Paul Brought Before Agrippa
- 26:19-23 Paul's Defense before Agrippa
- 25:1-12 Paul Appeals to Caesar

Paul Held in Cesarea
- 24:24-27 Paul Held Prisoner for Two Years
- 24:10-23 Paul Defends Himself before Felix
- 24:1-9 Paul Accused by Jews in Cesarea

27-28 Paul Goes to Rome

Shipwreck on the Way to Rome
- 27:13-20 The Storm
- 27:9-12 Paul's Advice to Delay Ignored
- 27:1-8 Beginning of Paul's Journey to Rome
- 27:21-26 Paul's Encouragement
- 27:27-38 Preparation for the Grounding
- 27:39-44 The Shipwreck

From Malta to Rome
- 28:1-22 Paul Speaks to the Leaders of the Jews in Rome
- 28:11-16 Paul Arrives at Rome
- 28:1-10 Paul Safe in Malta
- 28:23-31 Paul Preaches Jesus to Jews and Gentiles

Example: Matthew 5

I invite you to learn the key points of Matthew 5, as I did with Krishna in the plane.

You can see on this graphic the numbers 1–28, which represent each of the 28 chapters of the Gospel of Matthew. The background picture for this book is Moses holding the tablets of the law. This serves as a reminder that one of the pictures of Jesus is the new Moses—the prophet who would follow Moses, as announced in Deuteronomy 18:15–22. Through Moses came the first covenant, and through Jesus would come the new covenant. Accordingly, the title for the Matthew StudyMap is "New Covenant Through Jesus the Messiah."

The numbers 5–7, representing the chapters of the Sermon on the Mount, are positioned on the tablets of the law, to remind us that Matthew 5–7 is presented as the new law of the covenant that Jesus brought to us by perfectly following the first covenant.

Let us now focus on the first of these three key chapters, Matthew 5.

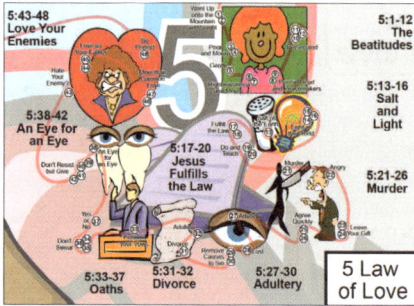

The title for Matthew 5 is "Law of Love."

The first part in the chapter is comprised of the Beatitudes (5:1–12), which is represented by the picture of a smiling, happy woman.

The second story is of salt and light, because in verses 13–16, Jesus invites us to be salt of the earth and light of the world.

The third story is found in the middle of the chapter picture because it is at the heart of chapter 5. In this story, we learn that Jesus fulfills the law (5:17–20). The picture is of two tablets, which serve as a reminder of the tablets of laws given to Moses.

The next story is about Jesus' teaching on the connection between anger and murder (5:21–26). Thus, the picture for this story features both an angry man and a man being stabbed to death.

The next story is about adultery; the image of an eye reminds us of the warning that lusting after a woman with our eyes is like committing adultery with her (5:27–30).

5:31-32 Divorce

The next story, to the left of the previous one, is about divorce (5:31–32), and the picture of a scroll reminds us of the letter of divorce.

Next, in verses 33–37, Jesus teaches that we should not make oaths; rather, our yes should be yes, and our no should be no. All that is added comes from the evil one.

5:33-37 Oaths

The picture of two eyes and two teeth reminds us of the verses on eye for eye and tooth for tooth (5:38–42), where Jesus teaches us to stop retaliating but rather be gracious.

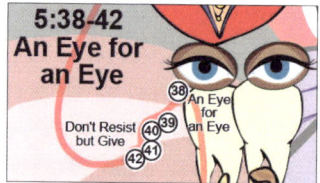

5:38-42 An Eye for an Eye

The last picture of the chapter is a heart with an aggressive face in the middle, which reminds us to love our enemies, as God loves the good and evil people, making

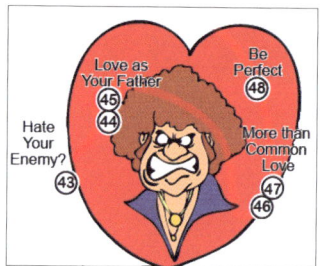

rain fall on each. The chapter then ends with an invitation to be perfect, as our Heavenly Father is perfect.

I invite you to look at the StudyMap of the whole chapter again, and to remember the position and title associated with each graphic. Once you can do that, I encourage you to try to remember, with your eyes closed, the stories from the last to the first, and then out of order. With this visual help, you will eventually be able to navigate your memory like a map—and that is one of the goals of the StudyMap approach.

6 Towards the StudyMap Learning Method

Learning to Pray

In 2013, on Réunion [RAY-oo-nyoh] Island, I tested the integration of the Bible StudyMap with theological classes by having students memorize the key stories of a Gospel. They learned how to playfully quiz each other, to be able to retell any story of a specific Gospel, including all the key points of each story. This StudyMap learning did not focus on rote memory but rather on accurate story points, so that each student would be able to learn, meditate on, and share Gospel stories with simplicity and accuracy. Since the focus was on key points, students could easily share this story in different languages, which is much more difficult after memorizing a text word-for-word. For instance, the students could learn the theme of each chapter of a book and the relative position of each chapter on the StudyMap, then the titles of key stories of specific chapters with their associated pictures. This would in turn enable them to recount each story with simplicity.

While we were serving on Réunion Island, I was asked if I would be willing to serve as the field strategy coordinator for the Central Field and the Indian Ocean islands near Africa. This meant overseeing the work of our denomination in this part of the world, and would involve more responsibilities and more travel. Sandra and I prayed about the opportunity and felt peace with it. I accepted the position and started in my new role in July 2013. Soon afterward, though, I began to realize I had a problem. The little church in Réunion had not grown during our ministry there—rather, it had shrunk. Now I was to oversee more than 300 churches! Would all these churches also shrink? I began to ask God in prayer, *What is the problem, Lord? What needs to change in me?*

One day soon afterward, I read a passage on prayer by Martin Lloyd-Jones, in which he mentioned that John Wesley used to say he thought very little of a man who did not pray four hours every day. I felt the Holy Spirit convicting me of my meager 15 minutes of daily prayer.

When I became a Christian, I wanted to better know God as revealed through His Word. I spent 10 years of my life in full-time theological studies. I learned extensively about important subjects like Biblical Hebrew and Greek, theology, counseling, and preaching. I spent hours every day studying Scripture, reading books, designing or improving StudyMaps, teaching others, and engaging in other ministry tasks. Yet prayer was very low in my priorities. I did not perceive the need to inform God of my situation and needs, since I rightly believed He already knew them. I viewed prayer as informing God. I had to learn that a key part of prayer is about encountering a gracious God, and listening to His loving guidance. As Jesus said, man shall not live by bread alone, but by every word that comes from the mouth of God.

At that point, I prayed a daring prayer. First, I told God that I was very busy with various ministry tasks—education, pastoring, designing graphic resources, and counseling—not to mention the important tasks of spending time with my wife and resting. So, I asked God, if He wanted me to pray more, to wake me up earlier so that I would have more time to pray. This was indeed a daring prayer, because we do have a living God! From September 2013, I began to wake up about four hours earlier each morning. I had to learn what to do during these hours, since I had very little experience in prayer. These early morning prayer hours would last more than a year, helping me to learn to integrate prayer into all I say and all I do.

> I had to learn that a key part of prayer is about encountering a gracious God, and listening to His loving guidance.

Slowly, I began to recognize more clearly the Holy Spirit's presence within me—what John Wesley called the "testimony of the Holy Spirit." I also noticed that people were more affected when I preached. One day, I asked God to confirm whether this was indeed His Spirit moving me when I preached. That same day, the leader of the Madagascar District told me that he sensed the presence of the Holy Spirit during the service as I spoke about the Lord. This encouraged me to move forward through prayer. With this praying for hours every morning, I noticed a new authority and discernment that allowed me to share words from God that were adapted to the people and situations I encountered.

In October 2013, before a trip to eastern DR Congo, I had the vision of a pile of weapons being brought into a church. I sensed that the vision was connected to my upcoming trip. I arrived there on 5 November 2013, and on 6 November, news outlets reported that the biggest guerrilla group in the area, the M23, had fled and left more than 300 tons of weapons behind.

I related the vision of the pile of weapons with this piece of news. I felt that God was doing amazing things and wanted me to play my part in His plan. It was as though He was asking me to serve as a "supporting character," while He acted as the hero of the story He was preparing in Congo.

In seeking to play my part, I prayed and asked for guidance on what to tell the people there. God made it clear to me that I should emphasize prayer and humility, and tell the people that He was bringing revival to eastern DR Congo. This message was very surprising to me, since the districts in eastern Congo had seen many crises and experienced tensions amongst their leaders.

Still, I joined the church there for a night of prayer. Together with the district leader in Goma, Jacques Balibanga [ZHAHK bah-lee-BAHN-gah], and two women of his district, we washed the feet of the meeting participants. Jacques ended up washing the feet of three of his major opponents. Together, we sought to model humility. After this night of prayer, those three opponents and the district board came to ask Jacques and me to perform another foot-washing at the district assembly. They also asked if the district leader could remain one more year so that they could more prayerfully prepare for his transition. From that day on, that troubled district became in many ways an exemplary district, and radiated a joy that other churches noticed. The Anglican and Baptist ministers present at our district meeting expressed their hope to see such a peace and joy impact their own church meetings. Many spoke of revival.

A few months later, we had to take medical leave because my dear wife Sandra was very tired and discouraged. What I did not realize then was that I did not know how to encourage her. I asked God in prayer to teach me to better listen to His voice and to give me words of encouragement for my wife. I then began to receive words in my heart, and I noticed that when I shared them with Sandra, they indeed encouraged her. I slowly realized that God not only knew my wife better than I did, but He could show me how to be a better husband. In this new process, I realized that, beyond the application of important biblical principles, I had not always allowed God to lead me. I began to dialogue with the Lord every day, not only speaking but also learning to listen to Him.

One of the things I felt the Lord asking me was to teach others to listen to Him. Since I was barely beginning to learn this myself, I thought this was a strange request. Still, I followed His voice and began to see miracles in many places.

The more I taught about listening to Him, the more the Lord helped me improve this teaching.

In Madagascar, a leader named Richard heard Jesus tell him that He would heal his leg cramps related to his diabetes—and indeed, Richard felt much better and emailed me about this experience a few days later. In Goma, during a night of prayer before an ordination, one participant heard Jesus say that He wanted to heal everyone there. We then prayed for many, and every person I prayed for said that their pain had disappeared.

In the last three years, Sandra and I traveled to more than 30 countries, speaking about how to integrate listening to God with sanctification and a joyful and holy walk with our Lord.

In the past, I had often wondered why I did not see the miracles that some ministers of the gospel described. The more I learned to spend time in prayer, to listen to the voice of my Shepherd and follow His guidance, the more I understood why: He is the one who does the miracles. When I did not humbly listen to Him, and therefore could not fully obey Him, it significantly limited the miracles of His love through me.

As I learn to follow His guidance more closely, I do see miracles, but I can only say, "I did what my Lord asked me to do," or "I said what my Lord asked me to say." This reminds me of what Jesus taught us in Luke 17:10, web: "We are unworthy servants. We have done our duty." It led me to a deeper understanding of what Paul teaches in Ephesians 2:8–10: "For it is by grace you have been saved, through faith—and this is not from yourselves, it is the gift of God—not by works, so that no one can boast. For we are God's handiwork, created in Christ Jesus to do good works, which God prepared in advance for us to do."

This inner revolution of prayer and of a life of intimacy with Jesus led me to a profound change in the way I practiced my faith. I felt led by the Lord to combine this listening to God with a study of Scripture using the StudyMaps. This led to what I now call the StudyMap learning method.

Meditating and Praying a Gospel Text

When we study Scripture, it is important to ask ourselves: What is my goal?

Is my goal to know more *data about God* or to *know God better*?

If we seek only to know more data, prayer becomes secondary in our priorities.

> Is my goal to know more data about God, or to know God better?

If our goal is to better know God and become disciples of Jesus, all the data we can learn is useful but only as a tool for intimacy and an obedient walk with God.

StudyMaps then become a tool to help us encounter God through Scriptures, to let God speak love to our hearts, and to guide us in showing this love in the world.

The goal of the StudyMap approach on the Gospels is threefold:

1. Learn to better know Jesus through the stories of the Gospels.
2. Learn to hear Jesus speak to us through the stories of the Bible and throughout our days.
3. Learn to dialogue with Jesus and follow Him all the days of our lives. As Jesus said, "My sheep listen to my voice; I know them and they follow me" (John 10:27, NLT).

There is one StudyMap of a Gospel text for each day of the year, starting with Matthew 1:1–17 on January 1, and ending with John 21:20–25 on December 31. These StudyMaps and the guide to use them are found on www.studymaps.org/Gospels.

The StudyMap for each day helps people remember a key Gospel story. This memory then helps us to meditate and allow God to speak in our specific situation.

It is good to first look at the whole Gospel chapter to see what the key stories are. You can then close your eyes and try to remember the pictures, their placement in the chapter, as well as the title for each story, as we did with Matthew 5 in the last chapter.

If you would like to enter this journey with the Study-Maps through the Gospels, I invite you to pray:

1. If you sense the need or desire to do so, commit your life to God and pray to be a disciple of Jesus. Repent of your sins, accept Jesus' sacrifice for your sins, and ask Him

to become your Lord and Savior. Then, invite the Holy Spirit to purify your heart, to fill you with His love and peace, and to guide you (Luke 11:13; Romans 5:5). If possible, ask a trusted Christian sister or brother to accompany you in this prayer.

2. Ask God if there is anything He wants you to change in your life. If whatever comes to your mind (picture, word, impression) makes sense with what you know of God, I encourage you to do what He shows you. If needed, ask the Lord for guidance on how to act. We don't worship a dead or distant God but a living and ever-present God. He knows every single hair on our head (Matthew 10:30).

3. Ask God if there is anyone you need to forgive, to remove the poison of unforgiveness from your relationship with God (Mark 11:25–26).

4. In following these steps, we are already beginning to listen to and follow God.

Then, as you interact with the StudyMap for each day:

1. Begin by committing your time to God, inviting His Holy Spirit to bring you peace and speak to you.

2. Look at the different parts of the story, following where the verses are located on the picture. Then close your eyes and try to remember the parts, their titles, and their positions in relation to the picture.

Example for January 2—Matthew 1:18–25: (Image on pg. 80)

- 18: Mary pregnant (on the right)
- 19–23: Joseph, don't be afraid (at the bottom)
- 24–25: Joseph named Him Jesus (top left)

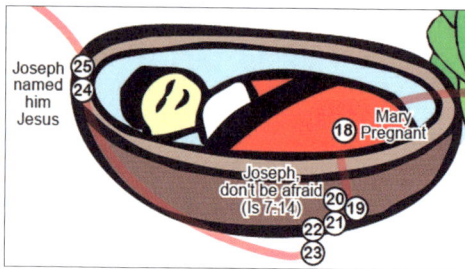

3. Read the text of the day without rushing, to help you focus. If you have a study Bible or other tools to help you understand the context of the passage, you can read those.

   If the story is one you can picture in your mind, close your eyes and imagine that you are part of the story. Picturing biblical stories in your mind and imagining that you are with Jesus in the stories (when possible) can help you learn to hear His voice. This method of visualizing the story was the way most people would listen to or read stories in biblical times. Letting God sanctify and use your imagination is also a way of becoming like a little child before Him (Matthew 18:3).

4. Ask Jesus if there is something He wants to tell you about the story you're reading, and listen to Him. Remember that Jesus promised His disciples that He would be with them until the end of the age (Matthew 28:20).

5. If what you heard from Jesus is coherent with what you know of Jesus—His love for you as a child of God and His character as the Son of God—apply what He tells you. If what you receive from God is unclear, don't hesitate to ask Him more about what He means or how to

apply what He says. Also, if you sense the need, don't hesitate to ask a mature Christian for help too. We have a very practical God, and He wants to guide us in practical ways so that we might have joy and bless others. Sometimes He speaks to us directly through prayer, and sometimes through other means (other people, nature, circumstances, etc.).

A key tool for discernment in these matters is the Wesleyan Quadrilateral,[8] which outlines the four key means through which God reveals himself: Scripture, tradition, reason, and experience. Please see the StudyMap version below:

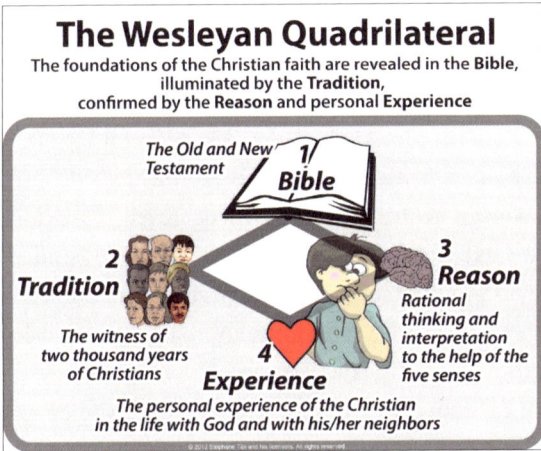

The Wesleyan Quadrilateral

The foundations of the Christian faith are revealed in the **Bible**, illuminated by the **Tradition**, confirmed by the **Reason** and personal **Experience**

The Old and New Testament
1 Bible

2 Tradition
The witness of two thousand years of Christians

3 Reason
Rational thinking and interpretation to the help of the five senses

4 Experience
The personal experience of the Christian in the life with God and with his/her neighbors

---

[8] The Wesleyan Quadrilateral, or Methodist Quadrilateral, is a methodology for theological reflection that is credited to John Wesley, leader of the Methodist movement in the late 18th century. The term itself was coined by 20th-century American Methodist scholar Albert C. Outler. This method based its teaching on four sources as the basis of theological and doctrinal development: scripture, tradition, reason, and Christian experience. (Wikipedia, adapted)

Explanation of the Methodology

God wants us to learn to live as His beloved children. We do this by following Jesus, the Son of God. We have to follow Jesus with all we are—with our head and our heart. We can remember here the most important commandment: "Love the Lord your God with all your heart and with all your soul and with all your mind" (Matthew 22:37).

Head

Definition: The head is associated with the mind's reasoning capacities, such as analysis and synthesis.

The head enables the scientific observation of an object, here the biblical text. When we study scriptures with the "head," we are the subject, and the text is the object of our study.

Limitations: Head knowledge is very useful for mastering a text. While it is necessary, it does not include encountering God. We can acquire head knowledge even if we don't believe in God. Studying with our heads helps us understand key ways God interacts with humans but does not lead us to such interactions. By itself, this approach can even lead us away from interactions with God.

Biblical roots: In the Hebrew language, the concept of "head knowledge" is often associated with the verb *bin* (בִּין) [BEEN] which in general means "to know, to discern." It denotes an analytical knowledge that allows us to separate and associate things.

Heart

Definition: The heart is associated with emotion, interaction, and the capacity to relate to others.

The heart helps us build relationships with others—here, a relationship with God through the Holy Spirit. When we learn to listen to and obey God through prayer, God is the subject, and He sees us not as objects but as persons with whom He wants a relationship.

Limitations: Without head knowledge, we will lack discernment, and it will be difficult to discern whether we are really hearing God speak to us or if we just speak to ourselves.

Biblical roots: For the "heart knowledge," the Hebrew uses the verb *yada* (עדי) [YAH-dah] which often implies intimate knowledge of another person.

The approaches of the head and the heart are very different but both are necessary.

Without heart knowledge of God, studying Scriptures is at best a pious practice—it will not transform us or lead us to be united with God in the way Jesus showed us through His life and actions.

> The approaches of the head and the heart are very different, but both are necessary.

Ultimately, the goal is to have our hearts and heads united as we learn to dialogue with God and follow Him in all we see and all we do. This is the way Jesus showed us; this is the way of disciples of Jesus. The purpose of the StudyMaps approach is to help you achieve this goal.

- Head: The StudyMaps and the memorization of key elements of the text help you understand the text and how the different parts relate to each other.
- Heart: The time you spend listening to Jesus through a specific text helps you develop a heart knowledge of God. When you feel that God has shown you something, ask Him questions. Jesus did not guide His disciples only by speaking *to* them but by interacting *with* them. Through the Holy Spirit, this is still true today. Jesus insisted that He is with us until the end of the age, through the Holy Spirit in us.

Jesus invites us to follow Him as our Lord and Savior, and to learn to be united with Him in both head and heart, with God, through Jesus' gospel of the Kingdom.

Listening to God and StudyMaps

The importance of biblical knowledge and a sound theological understanding cannot be overemphasized, especially in our modern world, where so many sources of information are available. Scripture is no longer the primary object of our meditation, as was the case in many Christian homes a few decades ago. It follows, then, that we need to develop practices and methodologies adapted to our electronic and visual age. That is the challenge that StudyMaps are designed to address.

It is very important to combine prayer with the study of Scripture. In doing so, we learn to better recognize the voice of God in Scripture and the guidance of the Holy Spirit in our everyday lives. This God-given recognition, in turn, allows us to live the joyful and holy lives to which we are all called.

I would like to illustrate the idea of a holy and joyful life with a recent story: In May 2017, I visited an educational leader from India named Simon. My predecessor, John, had built a strong and healthy relationship with him and his family, which allowed me to start from a gracious place. Simon and I quickly became friends.

Before lunch one Sunday, I spent time with Simon's oldest son, Solomon, who was 19 years old and pursuing a bachelor's degree in business in Bangalore. I had taught the first 6 articles of faith with the StudyMap at their church that morning. Since Solomon and his grandmother showed interest, I pulled my tablet out of my backpack, and used it to help them memorize the 16 Articles of Faith.

One thing I like to do when using StudyMaps with others is make the process like a game. If one person seems to be catching on quickly, I ask them to assume the role of the teacher. This lends a fresh and playful element to the work that helps everyone concentrate and learn even better.

Once Solomon and his grandmother had learned all the articles and understood them well, I invited them to close their eyes in prayer and ask God if there was anything He wanted to tell them concerning one of the articles. Solomon sensed the Lord telling him that he had spent too much time on Article 9 (justification) and needed to experience Article 10 (entire sanctification and Christian holiness). We prayed together, and in the coming days I saw Solomon take major steps in walking closer with the Lord. He was learning to recognize and honor the presence of the Holy Spirit inside him by following Jesus' guidance.

I then showed Solomon how to use the StudyMaps on the Gospels each day as a regular practice to develop intimacy with Jesus. Solomon proposed that he teach the remaining Articles of Faith to his church, since I had stopped at Article 6. Later that month, he did so—it was the first time he had preached. Solomon then began to use this StudyMap to teach the foundations of the Christian faith in other churches. He will soon travel to Sri Lanka to do the same there.

In September 2017, I was able to speak with Solomon about his continued journey with Jesus. I rejoice to see how honest and serious he is in discerning God's call on his life. Solomon and his father, Simon, have now begun to learn and meditate on the Gospel of Luke so they can use the StudyMap method to teach the book to others.

As you read these words, please join me in prayer for Solomon and his family, that through his life, he may bear beautiful and holy fruit for the Lord.

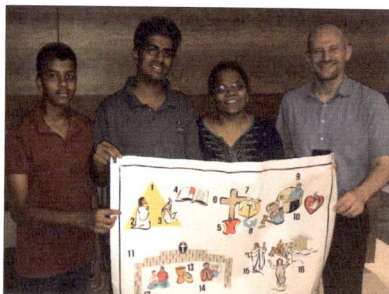

Solomon with his younger brother, his mother, and me.

Example: A Gospel Text—Matthew 5:13-16

In Matthew 5:13–16, Jesus said, "You are the salt of the earth. But if the salt loses its saltiness, how can it be made salty again? It is no longer good for anything, except to be thrown out and trampled underfoot. You are the light of the world. A town built on a hill cannot be hidden. Neither do people light a lamp and put it under a bowl. Instead they put it on its stand, and it gives light to everyone in the house. In the same way, let your light shine before others, that they may see your good deeds and glorify your Father in heaven."

There is no perfect method for learning to listen to Jesus—what is key is the faith and desire to know and follow Him. One way to listen to Jesus is to imagine that you are with Him in a peaceful place, and to ask Him, *Jesus, how do you want me to be the salt of the earth and a light in the world?*

I invite you to take a moment in prayer and listen to what He tells you. If it is in agreement with what you know of Jesus from Scripture, I encourage you to act on what He wants you to do. If His words to you are not yet clear, ask Him to show you more clearly what you can do in your present circumstances. Our Lord wants us to come to Him with the simplicity of a child.

Jesus is alive and well—let us learn to humbly listen to Him and do His will together!

7 Where Do We Go from Here?

As with any learning, if the teacher is a good role model, it impacts significantly the efficiency of the teaching. For instance, if as a teacher I want the students to be eager to learn, I need to show by example. This is why, when we teach the Articles of Faith, we try to learn the numbers and the name of each article in the local language, even if we sound a little awkward. In this case, the students from Bangladesh helped us to learn and pronounce correctly the name of each article. The fact that we showed interest for learning Bangla [BAYNG-lah] brought laughter and a much deeper fellowship, thus encouraging significantly our brothers and sisters to learn with us. This community approach to learning is an integral part of learning with StudyMaps.

The needs for training and discipleship are so numerous that the StudyMaps took off very well in Bangladesh. A month later, one of my colleagues was happy to see in Bangla a large print of the Articles of Faith and of Matthew 5.

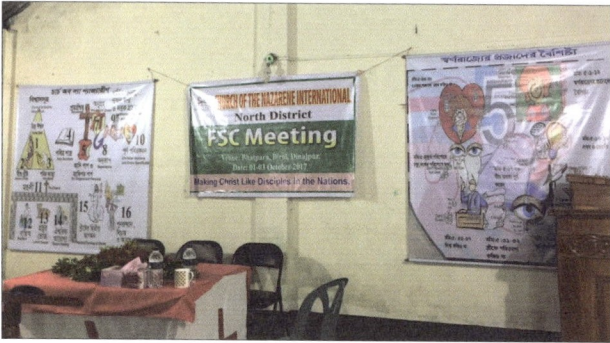

StudyMaps used for training in Bangladesh

We will work, in the coming months, on creative ways to use the StudyMap approach to support efficiently the training of as many pastors as possible in Bangladesh.

StudyMaps allow us to reach people everywhere and provide them a pathway towards a deep knowledge of Scriptures. This, in turn, opens the door to thorough training for ministry. In this way, the StudyMap approach is designed to train people of all literacy levels for efficient Christian service.

This approach encompasses three facets, all of which are intertwined in the learning process: 1. Self, 2. Neighbor, 3. God.

These facets reflect the foundational commands that Jesus describes in Mark 12:29–31: "'Hear, O Israel: The Lord our God, the Lord is one. Love the Lord your God with all your heart and with all your soul and with all your mind and with all your strength.' The second is this: 'Love your neighbor as yourself.' There is no commandment greater than these."

1. Self: Building relationships in the student's memory.

Often, in our education, we learn disjointed pieces of data. With StudyMaps, the purpose is not only to learn separate pieces of information but also to connect them in meaningful ways. StudyMaps foster not only a better memory of the facts but a building of meaningful relationships among them. The StudyMap on the Articles of Faith and the StudyMap on the books of the Bible serve as good examples of this function.

2. Neighbor: Building relationships between students.

This part of the process incorporates group learning methods with the StudyMap. It serves to connect the classroom by fostering love for the neighbor.

One of the possible learning strategies that can be incorporated with StudyMaps is Tell THE Story (a Sunday School and Discipleship Ministries International program that involves memorizing and learning Scripture together as a church body). Another possible example of this integration can be found in the guide to learning the Articles of Faith at www.studymaps.org.

Students then experience how they learn more efficiently in community than they do alone, and, therefore, discover a key value of being part of the Church, the Body of Christ.

3. God: Building relationship with God.

This third facet uses the first two as a solid foundation to teach people how to interact with God in prayer: by speaking to, listening to, and obeying God. This part of the approach helps students to understand and experience the relationship between sanctification (consecration and purification by the Holy Spirit) and listening to God (discerning God's communication and obeying God's guidance).

These three facets of the StudyMaps approach can be powerful tools in God's hands. He can use them to lead us and our communities in a revival of His love and in a renewed cultivation of scriptural holiness. This approach, used as a foundation for pastoral training classes, can then become the foundation for the discipleship that theological education requires.

As I continue to test and promote the StudyMaps, I like to challenge people to learn a Gospel using this method. Each step of the way I invite people to combine the three facets described above by employing the following principles:

1. Self: Aim to remember the key stories of the Gospel, the key stories of each chapter, the key points of each story, and the key points of each verse.

2. Neighbor: Learn in dialogue with others—in relationship with others. Encourage your study partners with playful quizzing and joyful interactions.

3. God: Each time you study, take time to bring your learning into your relationship with the Lord. Imagine yourself as a participant in the story you're studying. Ask Jesus to speak to you about what He would like you to learn from the passage. Then, put what He says into practice!

Spiritual Life and Biblical Knowledge

Learning Scriptures with StudyMaps, learning in community, and dialoguing with God in prayer have become a solid foundation of my walk as a disciple of Jesus.

When Jesus was on earth, He exemplified discipleship.

In Mark 3:14–15 we read, "[Jesus] appointed twelve that they might be with him and that he might send them out to preach and to have authority to drive out demons." In this text we notice three imperatives: 1. To be with Jesus, 2. To listen to and dialogue with Him, and 3. To do what He tells us. I like to think of these three imperatives as the model of discipleship. We can answer them by engaging in the following practices:

1. Prayerfully remain in the presence of Jesus—keeping the testimony of the Holy Spirit in us.
2. Carefully listen to Him in all the areas of our lives, through our study of Scriptures, and vibrant prayer lives.
3. Putting our faith into action by doing what He tells us to do.

I use this model to walk with others in their journey of discipleship. One of them, a dear brother who I will call M, lives in a country where it can be dangerous to be a

> Learning Scriptures with StudyMaps, learning in community, and dialoguing with God in prayer have become a solid foundation of my walk as a disciple of Jesus.

Christian. I met him a few months ago, and he is learning to be a servant of Jesus. We speak regularly, and I check in to ensure he is meditating on Scripture. I encourage him to use the StudyMaps method to increase his knowledge of biblical texts and develop an increasing sensitivity to the Holy Spirit so that he walks in holiness. M is a good example for many; he leads many youth towards a joyful walk with Jesus in a context that can be hostile. In such a difficult setting, memorizing Scripture is crucial. It helps M to continually meditate on God's teachings, wherever he is and whatever he does. Thus, he will better discern Jesus' voice in his everyday life.

I invite you to pray with me for M and the many others who live in places where Christianity is not accepted, that they may find efficient ways to carry Christ with them and to share His love and grace in the world.

Learning a Gospel

As this book comes to its end, I would like to challenge you to use a StudyMap to learn one of the Gospels. The best way to begin this process is to find a partner or a group of friends so that you can encourage one other as you learn together. Then, move forward step by step. You could begin, for instance, with the Gospel of the day (Matthew starts in January, Mark in April, Luke in June, and John in October), found on www.studymaps.org/Gospels. You might start by memorizing the title of each chapter with its relative position and the connection with the background picture. You can then progress one chapter at a time, making sure to remember the picture and title of each story. You can then learn the key points of each story, along with the position of the verse numbers on the associated picture. Finally, remember the key points of each verse.

When you come to this point for a specific story, I encourage you to close your eyes and imagine that you are part of the story. For instance, if the passage is the story of Jesus in the storm, you can imagine that you are with the disciples as the story unfolds. You can then ask Jesus, *Lord, what would You like to tell me concerning this story?* As you pray, listen for what Jesus wants to tell you. As long as what you hear is a clear manifestation of love for God or your neighbor, you can put it into practice with humility and faith. You will then have the opportunity to rejoice when this action brings good fruits, and to encourage each other to always more sensitively tune in to the teachings of the Lord, to be a faithful disciple of Jesus.

May our dear Lord Jesus bless you as you learn to serve Him, and as you learn to join the mission of God in our world.

This is the heart of StudyMaps:
to help people learn the
foundations of the Christian
faith, and thereby invite them
to come closer to our loving
Heavenly Father through His Son,
Jesus Christ.